SHROPSHIRE
THEN & NOW
IN COLOUR

David Trumper

For the staff of the Shropshire Records and Reach Centre, both past and present, for the wonderful work they do.

First published in 2011

The History Press
The Mill, Brimscombe Port
Stroud, Gloucestershire, GL5 2QG
www.thehistorypress.co.uk

British Library Cataloguing in Publication Data.
A catalogue record for this book is available from the British Library.

ISBN 978 0 7524 6320 9

Typesetting and origination by The History Press
Production managed by Jellyfish Print Solutions and manufactured in India

CONTENTS

ACKNOWLEDGEMENTS

I am indebted to Toby Neal, the Nostalgia Editor on the *Shropshire Star*, for his help, and I must acknowledge the information I have obtained from the many excellent articles on local history he has written for the paper over the years. I am also grateful for all the help and information I have received from the excellent staff at the Shropshire Records and Research Centre. My sincere thanks also goes to all the people who have loaned or given me photographs of the county, without which none of my books would have been possible. Last but not least my thanks go to my wife Wendy, who has accompanied me around the county, finding the correct angles to take the modern photographs and taking notes of locations, for proof reading the text and advising me on all aspects of the project.

ABOUT THE AUTHOR

Born in Shrewsbury, David Trumper worked as a printer for some years before training as a teacher, and taught at several Shropshire schools. Following his retirement, David has been able to pursue his interest in local history and photography and has collected and photographed over 20,000 views of Shrewsbury and Shropshire, dating from 1842 up until the present day. He has had eighteen books published and is well known around Shropshire for giving slide presentations and for leading historical walks. He has been married to Wendy for over forty years and has a daughter and two grandchildren.

INTRODUCTION

Shropshire is a large inland county, bordered by Wales on the west and by Cheshire, Staffordshire, Herefordshire and Worcestershire on the English side. It is a county of great diversity and its development has been influenced by countless generations from the Celts, Romans, Saxons and Normans through to the present day. The county is cut into two almost equal halves by the River Severn, which flows eastwards out of Wales and was once a major artery of trade and commerce through the county, being navigable for 150 miles from its mouth in Bristol to Pool Quay in Wales. To the north of the river is the Shropshire Plain, which stretches through into Cheshire and is blessed with rich farmland. Its landscape has been affected by glacial drifts, which formed the meres, Shropshire's own 'Lake District'. Whixall Moss close by is the county's fenland: an area rich in plant and animal life, which was saved in 1981 as a nature reserve. This relatively flat area is broken by sandstone ridges such as Nesscliffe, Hawkstone and Grinshill, and the area is full of ancient churches, buildings and bridges that have been built in this material. To the north-west the scenery is affected by the Welsh hills and the area becomes more Welsh in character and is full of Welsh names.

To the north-east is the Wrekin, which dominates the area from the edge of the plain. It is the second highest hill in the county, and was formed out of volcanic rock, although it was never a volcano. The area is also covered with seams of coal and deposits of limestone and iron ore, the basic ingredients that sparked off the Industrial Revolution in the area during the seventeenth century.

To the south of the River Severn lies the Shropshire hill country, a complete contrast to the north of the county. Around the Clun area are the round topped, undulating hills with pretty valleys merging with open heathland. There are the flat heights of the Long Mynd, the boulder-strewn peaks of the Stiperstones to the summit of the Clee Hills, the county's highest peaks, standing over 1,800ft above sea level. To the east of the Clee Hills is the Wyre Forest; while to the south-west are the remains of the old Clun Forest, parts of which ran into Wales.

The county is also enriched with a wide variety of habitations, from isolated farmsteads to large market towns. The two largest towns are Shrewsbury and Telford. Shrewsbury is the county town and dates back to around AD 901 when the first settlement was documented. Telford is a new town, conceived in the 1960s and built around the coalfields of East Shropshire, the birthplace of the Industrial Revolution. In the north are the market towns of Market Drayton, Wem, Whitchurch and Oswestry, where, until quite recent times, Welsh used to be the first language. In the south is Ludlow, described as 'the finest small town in the whole of England'. There is also Church Stretton, known locally as 'Little Switzerland', and Bridgnorth, once the county's second town.

Shropshire abounds in myths and legends, from the Devil's Chair to the Dunn Cow of Mitchell's Fold. The county has also bred numerous colourful and internationally renowned people, including 'Mad' Jack Mytton, Dame Agnes Hunt, Lord Robert Clive of India and Charles Darwin, author of *The Origin of Species*. The older photographs in this volume depict life in Shropshire throughout the twentieth century. The author took the modern views during March and April 2011.

PRIDE HILL

PRIDE HILL, SHREWSBURY, *c.*1950. This street takes its name from the Pride family who lived and owned property in the area during the reign of Henry III. At one time, one side of the street was known as the Shambles or Butchers' Row, while the other side was known as Corvisors' or Shoemakers' Row. In the old view the clock tower of the Victorian market hall stands proudly at the bottom of the hill. The street is also open to one-way traffic and the local family businesses of Affords, Maddox, Blower and Honeychurch are still trading in the main street.

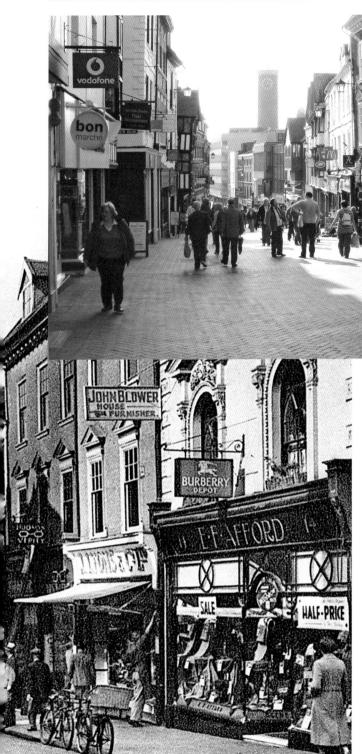

IN CONTRAST, THE new market hall and clock tower seem overbearing, as does the new Lloyds Bank. All the family firms have disappeared and been replaced by McDonald's, Past Times, Thornton's and Clinton Cards. Halfway down on the right is the entrance to the Pride Hill Centre, one of two large shopping centres opened in the town in the 1980s. The street was pedestrianised during the winter of 1982/83 for around £130,000 but on a busy weekday shoppers are endangered by delivery vans that still drive and park in the street.

MARDOL HEAD, SHREWSBURY

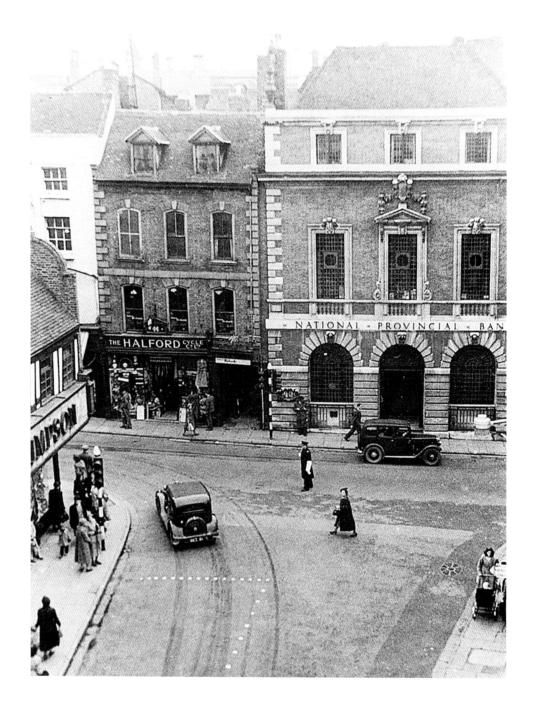

MARDOL HEAD, SHREWSBURY, *c.*1938 (left). This photograph was taken from the first floor window of Goodwin's Shop, by the owner H. R. 'Jim' Savage. The National Provincial Bank was built on that site in 1926 and moved there from Belstone. Halford's cycle and later car accessory shop occupied that site for well over half a century before moving to Castle Street and then out to the Meole Brace Retail Park. The passage between the shop and the bank is known as Plough Shut and once gave access from Mardol Head to The Square. On the left is Timpson's shoe shop. Although there are traffic lights, a police constable is still on traffic duty.

THE TOP OF Mardol has been pedestrianised, diverting all traffic down Claremont Street. Originally a raised flowerbed and benches were placed in the middle of the area but they have been replaced by a piece of modern art called Darwin's Gate. When viewed from a certain angle the three sections fit together to form a Saxon helmet and a Norman window. It cost £80,000 and was unveiled in November 2004 by the Mayor Councillor Miles Kenny. It caused a great deal of controversy with people complaining it was a 'Hideous Monstrosity' and that it should be shipped over to the Galapagos Islands!

ABBEY FOREGATE, SHREWSBURY

ABBEY FOREGATE, SHREWSBURY, c.1935 (above). Inspector Edwards reports back to the police station while on patrol in Abbey Foregate. He joined the Borough Force in December 1914 as PC 8. This view is looking up the street towards the Column. The timber-framed Cold Bath Court and Brook Street are on the right. The cottages and the larger house above were demolished in 1963 to make way for the new Safeway supermarket. Part of the tall building once housed an inn called the Barley Mow. Note the little boy in his go-cart and, just to his left, one of the town's conduits that supplied fresh drinking water to the residents of the town until the new water works was opened at Shelton in July 1935.

THE BUILDINGS ON the left have hardly changed and just a little white paint to doors and window frames brightens up their appearance. Abbey Foregate was once lined with trees and was referred to as the grandest entrance into the county town. Unfortunately many of the trees were removed in the early 1960s when the road was widened and upgraded to accommodate the A49, which also ran along Monkmoor Road and the newly opened Telford Way. The concrete and glass office blocks of the 1960s are visible to the right of the large chestnut tree in the centre. The new Netto Store, built in 2002 on the old Safeway site, is just above Cold Bath Court.

FORD

FORD, C.1910. The Pavement Gates Inn stands at the Shrewsbury end of the village on the main Welshpool road. The village lies just off the main road and a bridge has replaced the ford that gives the village its name. At the beginning of the twentieth century the inn belonged to William Vaughan, a draper, grocer, wine and spirit and ale and porter merchant, who lived at the White Horse Hotel in Worthen. It consisted of a kitchen, bar, two parlours, four bedrooms, a washroom and a cellar. The small brick extension behind the ducks is the gentlemen's urinal.

THE OLD INN was replaced around 1928; a former licensee recalls that if an inn closed in those days you lost your licence, so to avoid this the new inn was erected around the old one and they never officially closed. As soon as the new inn was finished the old one was removed. The new inn retained its old name until around 1980 when it was renamed the Owen Glendower, recalling the Welsh prince who climbed the Shelton Oak to watch the Battle of Shrewsbury in 1403 and was immortalised in Shakespeare's play *Henry IV*. Around 2007 it changed its name back to the Pavement Gates before being converted into an Indian restaurant called Saffron Cottage.

MONTFORD BRIDGE

MONTFORD BRIDGE, C.1910. There has been a bridge across the Severn at this point for hundreds of years. It was a traditional meeting point for two hostile races, the English and the Welsh, to gather and discuss their differences. Thomas Telford designed the present three-arched sandstone bridge in 1792 when he was constructing the new London to Holyhead Road. The building on the left with the porch is the Wingfield Arms, named after a local family who lived nearby at Onslow Hall.

TELFORD BUILT HIS bridge to the west of the old structure and at right angles to the river, which has produced sharp bends on the approach from both sides and is a hazard to modern motor traffic. The old sandstone balustrade of the bridge was replaced by metal barriers in 1963. The inn, which is still open, changed its sign to the Old Swan before reverting back to its former name. In 1901 C. N. B. Wingfield owned the inn and employed E. and J. B. Whitehorn to manage it. At that time the inn consisted of a bar, parlour, kitchen, clubroom, seven bedrooms, brew-house and cellar.

RUYTON-XI-TOWNS

RUYTON-XI-TOWNS, c.1935. The name of the village is derived from the old English 'ryge-tun' meaning a rye farm. The eleven townships that made up the manor were Ruyton, Shotatton, Eardiston, Coton, Shelvock, West Felton, Wykey, Haughton, Sutton, Rednal and Tedsmore. Ruyton was deliberately created by the Fitz Allen family in the thirteenth century, was granted a charter in 1308 and remained a Municipal Borough until 1886. The photographer is looking up School Road

towards Wykey. The tall building on the left is Compton House, while just beyond is a white building that was removed sometime after the Ruyton Co-operative Dairy was established at the end of the Great War.

IN OUR MODERN view, road markings and signs show that the automobile has taken the place of the sheep. The cross was unveiled in April 1881, some thirty years after it had been suggested that a cross with a light and a drinking fountain should be erected on the site of the old village lock-up. The drinking fountain never materialised and there were many complaints from villagers that the light was never lit. The house on the right with white walls is Smithy House, the home for many years of the blacksmith Edward Lloyd. The old farm buildings behind the cross have been replaced by a modern house.

BAILEY HEAD, OSWESTRY

BAILEY HEAD, OSWESTRY, *c.*1935. The Bailey is the site of the town's open market and the name recalls the castle built by the Normans, the remains of which stand behind the Guildhall on the left. The Guildhall, with its highly ornamented front, was designed by H. A. Cheers of Twickenham and was built in 1893, costing in the region of £11,000. It replaced an older

hall erected in 1782 on the site of the Wool Hall. To the right is Powis Hall, built in the Georgian style in 1839. The building once housed the corn exchange and the cheese and butter market. The children are playing round the Bailey Head Pump, which was installed in 1776.

THE BAILEY HEAD is still the centre of a flourishing weekly market. The restored Guildhall stands proudly on the left, but the old Powis Hall was demolished and replaced in 1963 by this building, which at the time won great praise for its architecture! A plaque on the building states 'Oswestry, – Powis Hall. Reconstructed by the Corporation of Oswestry and opened 11th September 1963, by Col. The Right Hon. The Earl of Powis CBE TD DL, whose predecessor gave the original building in 1839.' Another plaque refers to a container that was buried beneath the building by the Mayor Councillor T. Bain on 4 March 1978 to commemorate the Queen's Silver Jubilee. The pump was removed in 1958 and has been replaced by a flower display stand.

THE CROSS, OSWESTRY

THE CROSS FACING Willow Street, 1960 (right). A variety of businesses were located in this area of the town. On the left is the Midland Bank, erected in 1890, with Llewellin's chemist shop next door. The last shop before Willow Street is Phillips' Store, which had outlets throughout the county; in the nineteenth century it was an inn known as the Golden Eagle. The first shops in Willow Street were Peterwood Ltd, selling casual wear, and Dale Brothers, furniture dealers. On the white wall on the corner you can see part of the sign for the business of James Waterworth and Son, fruiterers and greengrocers. Coming back to the Cross we have Grant's Arcade on the right and part of the Cross Market, built in 1842 and housing Willson's ladies' and children's outfitters.

A NEW ROAD layout has been established and the unsightly island removed, giving a better view into Willow Street. The Midland Bank has become the HSBC and has extended its building on to the site of Llewellin's chemist shop. This wider view shows the cross on the right that once

stood on the site of the traffic island. It was erected in 1862 by Henry Bertie Watkin Williams Wynn and bears the legend 'The Fear Of The Lord Is The Fountain Of Life'. It once stood 11ft high but was removed in 1882 to the Castle Bank after being damaged on several occasions. It was restored close to its original site when the roads were restructured.

SCOTLAND STREET, ELLESMERE

SCOTLAND STREET, ELLESMERE, c.1920 (right). Lloyds Bank occupied this corner for well over a hundred years. Just beyond is the Victoria Commercial Hotel, which was once known as the Bull and Dog. The building with the magnificent portico, and Ionic pillars that straddled the pavement, is the Black Lion. It was the larger of the two inns around 1900 with seven rooms on the ground floor and sixteen upstairs. The large building at the top of the street is the post office. Opposite the Black Lion is the Savings Bank, which was purpose-built in 1830 at a cost of £360.

THE NARROWNESS OF the street and the increase in road traffic are illustrated in the need for double yellow lines and for the priority traffic sign giving right of way to vehicles travelling up the road. The portico outside the Black Lion has also gone; it was removed after being made unsafe by milk lorries bumping it while negotiating the sharp turn into Wharf Road. Before modern transport blocked up our towns there was stabling for eighteen horses at the rear of the Victoria and for forty at the Black Lion. The Victoria Hotel has closed though the iron frame to support the inn sign remains on the wall; it is now the Coco Coffee Bar.

ST JOHN'S HILL, ELLESMERE

ST JOHN'S HILL, Ellesmere, *c.*1920. Two postmen, a man with a bike and three youngsters pose for the photographer at the junction of the hill and Birch Road. The butcher's shop on the

corner belonged to John Copnall who was also listed as a farmer at Sandy Hill. Other residents of St John's Hill at this time were Miss Emma Drover the mistress of St John's Hill School and Burton Buckley who ran a confectionery shop at No. 5. There were once two public houses on the hill, the Three Tuns at No. 6 and the George and Dragon, but both were closed before 1900.

THE COPNALL FAMILY sold meat from here for over fifty years, previous to which they had a shop in Market Street and were also licensees of the White Lion. Their shop is now a private house, the cobbles have gone and the other cottages on the hill are now all used for residential purposes. The three-storey terraced houses were built between 1810 and 1839, replacing a number of timber-framed buildings. The road, being extremely narrow, was not made for modern traffic but parking is still allowed and the road is still open for two-way traffic.

THE WAR MEMORIAL, WEM

THE WAR MEMORIAL, Wem, 19 December 1920. The 14ft-high memorial, built out of Portland Stone, was erected in the churchyard between the north-east door of the church on the left and the Union Buildings on the right. It was unveiled by Brig.-Gen. H. C. Cholmondely and dedicated by the Revd the Hon. A. Parker. The hymn 'Peace, Perfect Peace' concluded the ceremony, after which a large number of floral tributes were placed on the memorial by family and friends of

those who sacrificed their lives in the First World War. At the time of the unveiling, the memorial had the names of fifty-six local men who had fallen in the First World War inscribed upon its octagonal base.

THE UNION BUILDINGS were erected around 1831 to tidy up the area and widen the High Street. There was a row of shops on the ground floor and a room above that was used for a time as a reading room. The building was removed in 1941 so that the High Street and the corner could be widened to suit modern traffic. The demolition opened up the area and a fine view of the north side of the church. The steps and gateway on the left with the ornate lamp have been removed and a new entrance has been made from the High Street. The building at the rear is the Parish Hall.

HIGH STREET, WEM

HIGH STREET, WEM, 1960 (right). Hall, Wateridge & Owen Ltd the local firm of auctioneers, valuers and estate agents, had this office at No. 3 High Street, opposite the junction with New Street. These buildings with their quaint cobbled forecourt were once part of the Talbot: one of the town's posting houses. It was first licensed around 1820 and in 1896 it had five rooms on each floor. One of the rooms on the ground floor was used as an office for William Hall's brewery. The building just across the road to the left is the White Lion that was first recorded around 1840. Note the dog sitting patiently in the shade.

THE OLD BUILDINGS were knocked down a number of years ago and this modern structure, which is now Wem Library and Learning Centre, put up in its place. The building also houses part of Walford and North Shropshire College. The road to the side of the White Lion leads to the town's main car park. The White Lion is still open as a public house. In a survey in 1896 the inn had stabling for ten horses and although part of the stables were in a very poor state, new accommodation was about to be put up. The auctioneers, now known as Halls, have closed their Wem branch and their nearest office is in Ellesmere.

SHAWBURY

SHAWBURY, C.1930 (right). The photographer is looking down the A53 towards Market Drayton with Church Road on the right. The building on the left is the Elephant and Castle Hotel. It was originally a three-storey dwelling erected in 1734 by Sir Walter Corbet. In 1901 it was listed as having eight rooms on the ground floor, ten rooms upstairs and stabling for eighteen horses. William Pinnock was running the shop in 1921 but by 1937 it had been taken over by Archibald Pinnock. In 1937 the garage belonged to William Foulkes. He was listed in 1921 as a cycle manufacturer, blacksmith and implement maker, and 'sole maker of the Maypole cycle'.

THE DOORS OF the Elephant and Castle are still open for guests, and the building with the Hovis sign that housed Pinnock's shop still stands although the shop has shut and the building is now occupied by Gareth Jones, a chartered certified accountant. A new Texaco garage was built on the site of William Foulkes' garage although part of the old structure remains and has been incorporated into the Great Wall Chinese and Cantonese takeaway. The Texaco garage has also closed and is now occupied by Simons of Shropshire Quality Car Centre and a Co-operative Society store.

HODNET

HODNET, C.1900. The village is a Celtic settlement and its name is derived from Hodnant, meaning a peaceful valley. The village huddles around the church and has many fine examples of timber-framed houses. The octagonal tower of the Church of St Luke is visible through the eaves of the houses. The tower is the only one of its kind in the county and dates from the fourteenth century.

The fine thatched cottage in the centre is known as Ye Hundred House. In days gone by the villagers elected their own coroner on the steps of this house and on fair days home-brewed beer was sold there. The village was first granted a charter to hold weekly markets and an annual fair during the reign of Henry III.

YE HUNDRED HOUSE has changed little over the years although it has lost its thatched roof and now has two extra dormer windows. The elaborate gas lamp to the right of the house has also been removed. The cottage to the left with the fine barleycorn chimney stacks is now occupied by the Mulberry Studio. Road markings and signs are evident but since 2006 a new bypass has been built to take heavy traffic away from the historic centre of the village. Hodnet Hall, the home of the Heber-Percy family, stands close by and is a popular tourist attraction.

PREES

PREES, C.1910. This view at the crossroads is looking towards Whitchurch, with Mill Street on the left and Church Street on the right. The name of the village is Celtic and means brushwood. In the eighteenth century it was an important coaching stop where horses could be changed and

travellers fed and rested, and at one time the village had twelve inns to cater for the coaching trade. Only the New Inn, the white building on the right past the crossroads, survived. Archibald Bradbury ran the butcher's shop on the corner of Church Street for many years. On the immediate right is a branch of the United Counties Bank. The house with the bay windows on the left is Devonshire House, while the three-storey building beyond the New Inn is Prees House.

DURING THE LATTER half of the twentieth century the busy Shrewsbury to Whitchurch road became so congested in the narrow main street through Prees that a bypass was built, which brought great relief to the village. The old bank is now empty and run-down, and the butcher's shop has been converted into a dwelling. The house on the opposite corner has also been renovated and the timbers, hidden by pebbledash on the old print, have been revealed. The New Inn has also closed, leaving the village without a public house.

WATERGATE, WHITCHURCH

WATERGATE, WHITCHURCH, 1960. The photographer is looking towards the junction of Mill Street and Castle Hill. The white building at the bottom is the Swan Hotel. It was an old coaching inn with parts of it dating from the seventeenth century. There was stabling at the rear for a

hundred horses and in the early 1800s the
Manchester coach departed from there at 8 a.m.
On the opposite side of the road is the sign of
the Bull Ring Vaults. The inn commemorates
the barbaric sport of bull baiting held in an area
between Watergate Street and the High Street and
last practiced in the town in 1802.

IN THE MODERN view the Swan has been replaced
by a new building erected in 1971 by Tesco as the
town's first supermarket. Tesco only stayed there
fifteen years before moving to larger premises.
Argos and Ethel Austin now occupy the building.
The Bull is still trading and has been licensed for
nearly 200 years. In August 1894 the landlord was
convicted of selling adulterated brandy for which
he was fined 6d plus 29s 6d costs. The Watergate
Hardware Store has closed and a number of shops
have been converted back to dwellings. The three
people on the right are walking past the entrance
to a small arcade of shops.

WHITCHURCH

WHITCHURCH IN 1960. The name is derived from White Church and the town has been identified as the site of the Roman town of Mediolanum, situated on the road from Uriconium (Wroxeter) to Chester. Bowen's Ltd sold ladies' and children's clothes, a variety of haberdashery

and household furnishings; they started trading in the town in about 1920. This is the junction of High Street, Green End and the Bull Ring. At this time cars were still allowed to park in the centre of town and to travel down Watergate towards Wrexham, Newport and Shrewsbury. Note the road signs on the side of Bowen's shop.

BOWEN'S AND BOOTS' stores have both gone and the High Street and Green End were converted to one-way traffic when the Bull Ring and Watergate were pedestrianised in 1994, a move that caused some controversy at the time. The clock, marking the completion of this and other work in the town, was made by Joyce's, who have manufactured clocks in the town for over 200 years. Under each of the four clock faces are the names the town has been known by during its 2,000 year history: Roman Mediolanum, Saxon Westune, medieval Album Monasterium and modern Whitchurch.

MARKET DRAYTON

MARKET DRAYTON, C.1900. This market town in north Shropshire is largely unspoilt and has a full range of shops and services. The Church of St Mary dates mainly from the fourteenth century. It is a large church and was heavily restored by the Victorians. As a boy Robert Clive, who was born nearby, is said to have climbed the outside of the tower, a feat that would have taken great courage, a quality he would have needed in his later life in India. The watermill was one of nine around Market Drayton that used the waters of the River Tern as a source of power.

THE MODERN VIEW taken from the Meadow shows the church in all its glory now that the trees that once obscured it have been removed. The watermill has gone and its site now occupied by Janes Beverage Ltd and an electrical sub station. Just in front of the tower is a large memorial, the roof of which is supported by four Corinthian pillars. It is dedicated to William Beeston, a surgeon who practiced in Wellington and died in March 1846. It was commissioned by his niece, Tabitha Beeston, who was also interred there in May 1854.

SHROPSHIRE STREET, MARKET DRAYTON

SHROPSHIRE STREET, MARKET Drayton *c.* 1920. The large Georgian house between the timber-framed cottages is Poynton House. It was designed by an unknown architect and built for

George Warren in 1753. He was related to the Warren Family who lived at Warren Court, a property to the left of the cottages at the top. The Warrens were solicitors and lived there for over 150 years. During the 1820s sheep stealing was a major crime in the area and Charles Warren helped to apprehend one of the leading gangs, known as the Bravos. After the trial two of the gang were hanged and three were transported to Australia.

THOMAS JONES REMOVED the top cottages in the 1930s when he opened a garage at Warren Court and needed the space for a forecourt. Warren Court, erected in the early 1700s, was once known as the Manor House. It was refronted in 1778 and converted into flats in 1987. The thatched cottages on the right have also been partly demolished and rebuilt in a similar style. Note the signs over the doors in the old view advertising John Darbyshire, a bootmaker, in the centre and Ye Olde Grocery Shoppe to the left.

STAFFORD STREET, MARKET DRAYTON

STAFFORD STREET, MARKET Drayton, 28 November 1969 (right). The ladies are coming out of Stafford Street into High Street. The building on the corner was demolished to widen the road and make access for larger vehicles easier into the High Street. The white building on the left is the Crown, one of the houses not destroyed in the great fire of 1651 when 140 buildings were burnt to the ground. According to local tradition, King Charles I is reputed to have slept at the inn during the Civil War. In 1887 the landlord was taken to court and fined 24s 6d for selling intoxicating liquors on unlicensed premises.

THIS WIDER VIEW of the corner shows the timber-framed front of the Crown running along Queen's Street. The inn once had its own brewery at the rear that was dominated by a huge chimney stack. In 1901 the inn was described as 'very old but in fair repair. Stabling out of repair.' The corner has been tidied up and attractive seating has been provided. The building that was shored up is now the Britannia Building Society Office and just below in Stafford Street is the Spicy Corner Tandoori, Balti Curries and fast food takeaway. The building in which it is housed was erected in 1910.

HIGH STREET AND
LOWER BAR, NEWPORT

HIGH STREET AND Lower Bar, Newport, 1960 (left). Lower Bar begins at Hogben's Garage on the left. The business was started in the 1930s and by the 1960s they were agents for Austin, Ford and Singer cars. The shop next door is the Canister Shop – note the canister over the door. It was famous for its selection of cheeses and was run by the Midgley family from about 1920 until 1983. On the right is the Swan Inn, which was first licensed at the beginning of the nineteenth century. In a survey in 1901 it was reported that the 'house requires renovating throughout'.

HOGBEN'S GARAGE HAS gone and the building is now occupied by Home Essentials. Next door is now Salters Court and half of the Canister is still a shop, while the other half is a private dwelling. The large building on the left is Roddam House. Across the road the Swan Inn is still open but has changed its name to the Newport Arms. The biggest change is that the buildings on the corner of Salters Lane have been demolished and a large petrol station and garage has been built on the site.

TOWN HALL, NEWPORT

HIGH STREET, NEWPORT, 1960. The large building on the right is Newport Town Hall. The architect was J. Cobb and it was erected in 1860 in a style described by Pevsner as debased Italianate. It was paid for by the Newport Markets Company, cost about £13,000, had two large assembly rooms capable of holding 250 and 500 people and provided space for the town's general markets, held on a Friday. By the 1960s many residents thought it was an eyesore and in a heated debate held to discuss its future one speaker labelled it 'a monstrosity'. The Vine

Vaults on the left was first licensed in the early years of the nineteenth century with accommodation of eight rooms on the ground floor and another thirteen on the first floor.

THANKFULLY THE DEMOLITION men were not sent in and the town hall was completely renovated in 1964. Sadly the Vine Vaults did not receive the same treatment and was demolished early in 1966 and replaced by a typical 1960s building. It reopened as The Vine before changing its name to The Village and then to Main Street. Today it is the Vine Central Square Nightclub with a 'Challenge 25' entry policy. To the right of the Vine Vaults is St Mary's Lane, named after a chapel in the church, and the road going off to the right is Stafford Road.

THE TALBOT INN, NEWPORT

HIGH STREET, NEWPORT, *c*.1905 (right). The photographer has his back to Upper Bar and is looking down High Street towards the town hall. The road is wider at this point and there are some fine residencies on both sides of the road. The building on the left facing down the road is the National Provincial Bank, which was housed in that building before the end of the nineteenth century. The Trustees Savings Bank opened an office immediately behind them at No. 21. The three-storey building to the left was an inn called the Talbot. The Talbot is a breed of dog and is the emblem of the Earls of Shrewsbury. There are mentions of an inn on that site in 1641.

THE COBBLES HAVE gone and the trees have been replaced by modern street furniture. The road has also been narrowed and the pavement on the right widened. The National Provincial Bank has amalgamated with the Westminster Bank to become the National Westminster and the old bank buildings and the houses to the left have been demolished and a new office built to take their place. The Talbot Inn has closed and is now known as The Literary Institute Town House. The Institute was founded in 1883 and moved to these premises in 1927.

BRADFORD STREET, SHIFNAL

BRADFORD STREET, SHIFNAL, *c.*1910. All the buildings on the left were built over the medieval market place. The property with the tower is the Market Hall, known to the locals as the town hall. It was built out of red brick and contained a spacious room, capable of holding 330 people for public meetings. Before the First World War it was used by the Territorial Army as a drill hall and for dances and concerts up until the 1950s. The British Workman on the right was a temperance hotel and coffee tavern until about 1917. Before this it was a library and free reading

room donated by Mr and Mrs H. Maclean of Aston Hall. Further along, behind the gas lamp, is the sign of the Talbot Inn.

BRADFORD STREET COMMEMORATES the Earls of Bradford whose ancestral home, Weston Park, lies close by, straddling the Shropshire-Staffordshire border. All the buildings on the left of the old photograph were demolished in 1966 and quite a number on the right-hand side, which makes the scene quite unrecognisable. The demolition opened up the road on the other side of the Market Hall that was known as Cheapside. Until recently HSBC bank occupied the site of the British Workman but today the spot is occupied by PC Doctor and the Carpet Gallery.

RAILWAY BRIDGE AND MARKET STREET, SHIFNAL

BRADFORD STREET, SHIFNAL, *c.* 1960. This view is looking towards the railway bridge and the Market Square. Thomas Lloyd had opened a grocery shop in Church Street by 1885 and had moved

to Park Street ten years later. By 1900 John Charles Lloyd had taken the business over and he added other branches to the firm in the Market Square and this shop in Bradford Street. Just below is the jeweller's and watch repairer's belonging to John Cheadle and on the corner of Aston Street is Barclays Bank. The buildings on the right lie empty and await demolition.

J. C. LLOYD'S SHOP has been replaced by a modern building but Barclays Bank is still trading on the corner. The buildings on the right were demolished in 1966 and the open aspect gives a better view of the railway bridge through to the Market Square. The original was a handsome arched bridge that was cast by the Horseley ironworks in Tipton and erected in 1848 to connect the Shrewsbury to Birmingham line. It was rebuilt in this style in 1953 when the old structure was considered unsound and could no longer be insured.

NEW STREET, WELLINGTON

NEW STREET, WELLINGTON, 1960 (below). The 'new street' was laid out in 1244. From the far end of the street we have Johnson's the dry cleaner's, Baxter's the butcher's, Craddock's shoe shop and Frank Burton's chemist shop. He opened his first shop at No. 52 New Street in the 1920s but had moved to these premises by 1934. F. W. Woolworth arrived in the town towards the middle of the twentieth century, while the electrical shop of E. W. Jones was occupied in 1968 by John James, who sold radios and televisions.

LIKE OTHER STREETS in Wellington, the car has been banned and the road pedestrianised for the convenience of the shopper. All the buildings are the same except for the one on the extreme

right and the one to the left of the Woolworth building whose dormer windows have been replaced. This branch of Woolworth closed in 2008 when branches around the country ceased trading due to the financial crisis. The property is now occupied by Heron Foods who advertise 'Top Quality Lowest Prices'.

MARKET STREET, OAKENGATES

MARKET STREET, OAKENGATES, *c*.1930 (right). At the beginning of the nineteenth century there was only a very small settlement here but with the arrival of the railway, which raised its profile and made it more accessible, a thriving town soon developed. By 1854 the main street boasted a full range of shops and other amenities, which included a number of public houses. The second house on the left is the Oxford Hotel, which at this time was owned by Lichfield Brewery. Next door is the butcher's shop of Albert Spendlove Grateley and beyond there is Lloyds Bank and Baker's shoe shop.

TWO OF THE shops on the left, in the centre of the row, have been replaced by modern buildings, compared with the majority on the other side that have been rebuilt. The hotel closed and was tenanted by Lloyds Bank before being occupied by Clarkes Solicitors. Although the street is only open to one-way traffic, cars parking on both sides of the road often make life difficult for pedestrians and other road users. The railway bridge taking the Shrewsbury to Birmingham line over the road can be clearly seen in the distance on both views.

HIGH STREET, DAWLEY

HIGH STREET, DAWLEY, 1960 (left). The township of Dawley moved away from the old parish church to this area early in the nineteenth century. Any type of roadworks in Dawley High Street caused absolute chaos, as the busy narrow road was still open to traffic travelling in both directions. Pedestrians take great care as they negotiate the hazards on the pavement or try to cross the road and a police officer monitors the situation from the roadside. The inn on the right is the Talbot, which was first recorded in 1846. Early in the twentieth century you could enjoy a pint of the landlord's home-brewed beer and play a game of snooker or billiards.

SOME NEW BUILDINGS have been erected on the left but, apart from some minor alterations to shopfronts, most of the properties remain the same. On 12 September 1980 a boost was given to the people of Dawley when comedian Ken Dodd opened a new pedestrianised High Street. Traffic was diverted around the town on the Dawley Greenway and three good car parks were provided, giving easier access to the town centre. This year, 2011, the centre has again been rejuvenated and the whole of the High Street re-laid.

BRIDGE STREET, HORSEHAY

BRIDGE STREET, HORSEHAY, *c.*1930 (right). The Horsehay Works was once part of the Coalbrookdale Company but was sold off in the 1880s. The factory was taken over by H. C. Simpson and his brother, who were from Rotherham. Later the factory was owned by Adamson & Butterley and then by AB Cranes before closing in the 1980s. They were famous throughout the world for building cranes and bridges. The famous Sentinel Steam Waggon was developed there between 1900 and 1903, before finding a permanent home in Shrewsbury.

UNTIL THE MIDDLE of the eighteenth century Horsehay

was a farmstead and a few scattered cottages. Abraham Darby II rented some land there to build a blast furnace in 1754 and in 1756 a brick works was also in operation. Today most of the factory has been demolished, but this section, which housed the design shop and other offices, has survived and is now occupied by a firm called Horsehay Limited Offices and Warehouses. In the 1990s the space left by the factory was redeveloped with modern housing and the village now has more of a rural feel to it.

HIGH STREET, IRONBRIDGE

HIGH STREET, IRONBRIDGE, *c.*1900. The world's first cast-iron bridge is just out of sight on the left. The buildings on the junction of Church Hill are the Municipal Buildings. On the right is the purpose built ironmonger's shop belonging to Frank Beddoes. As well as selling all the usual hardware he was also a blasting powder, fuse and dynamite merchant. The boys are looking with great interest into the window of James Simpson's music shop. At the top of the hill is the Church of St Luke, erected in 1836 and consecrated the following year. On Census Sunday

in 1851 the morning service attracted 500 adults and 80 children and at evensong the congregation was 700.

QUITE A NUMBER of buildings have been removed from both sides of the road. The cast-iron gas lamp, made at Coalbrookdale, has been re-sited to the side of Nock Deighton's office on the left and its place taken by a mini traffic island. The lamp was erected by public subscription in 1898. Nick Tart the estate agent now occupies the ironmonger's shop. Where the Union Buildings stood is a small garden dedicated to the Rotary Club of Ironbridge on their Golden Anniversary in 2005. Interesting additions to the new view are the cooling towers belonging to Buildwas Power Station that can be seen through the trees in the centre.

THE SQUARE, MUCH WENLOCK

THE SQUARE, MUCH Wenlock, 1960 (right). This picturesque little town is famous for its ancient priory dedicated to St Milburga, and its name is thought to derive from the Celtic *gwen-loc*, 'white monastery'. The town is also famous as the birthplace of the modern Olympics. A local doctor, William Penny Brookes, founded the Wenlock Olympian Society in 1850. Early games included such events as the wheelbarrow race, but as the games became more athletic they attracted wider interest, leading to the first international games being held in Athens in 1896. The building on the corner of The Square and High Street is the post office and just above is the George and Dragon.

WITH 2012 AND the London Olympics fast approaching, the town is preparing for an influx of tourists. The growing

recognition of Penny Brookes' influence on the Olympic movement has been enhanced with the naming of one of the Olympic mascots 'Wenlock'. Since 1960 The Square has been given a facelift: new buildings have been erected on two sides with small shop units on the ground floor. The area has also been paved and seating provided. The clock was erected to celebrate Queen Victoria's Diamond Jubilee in 1897 and the mayor, Mr Thomas Cooke, unveiled it. It was completely restored in 1993 to celebrate the fortieth anniversary of our present Queen's accession to the throne.

CROSS HOUSES

CROSS HOUSES, C.1935. The photographer is looking back towards Shrewsbury on the main road from Bridgnorth to the county town. Two sisters, Edith and Minnie Machin, ran the shop on the left. As well as groceries the sisters offered travellers teas and refreshments as well as catering for bed and breakfast. Almost opposite is the sub-post office and just beyond the houses on the right is the Fox Inn, which is probably the oldest building in the village. There is also another inn, the Bell on the opposite side of the road. Further along the road is the Atcham Union Workhouse that survived until the First World War when it was converted into a military hospital, and after the war it continued to serve the county as a general hospital.

THE VILLAGE HAS changed beyond
all recognition and you have to
look carefully to recognise that the
white house on the right and the one
directly behind but slightly to the left
are all that remain of the buildings in
the old photograph. The buildings on
the left were demolished so that the
road could be straightened and made
wider. The hospital closed in 1987 and
was converted into offices. Now only
part of the hospital remains as the
site has been developed into a housing
estate. Note the neat brick bus shelter
on the left.

WORFIELD

WORFIELD, C.1935. Two cyclists ride down the middle of the road and not a car in sight. This
quiet, picturesque village lies four miles north-east of Bridgnorth between a steep sandstone ridge

and the River Worfe, which gives the settlement its name. The Church of St Peter, built in the thirteenth century, dominates the village with its elegant fourteenth-century spire that rises to a height of 200ft. On the left is the Davenport Arms, which is known locally as The Dog. Further down the street, behind the telegraph pole on the left, is the village store, run for many years by the Clark family.

THE VILLAGE INN and store are still functioning, but the main street is much more congested with traffic. Just before the red telephone kiosk, set back off the road are a small block of modern flats erected in 1966. Most of the land in the area belongs to the Davenport Estate and their tenants still have to report to the inn twice a year to pay their rent. The inn was first licensed around 1800. In 1901 the owner was Mrs Davenport but it was occupied by George Eden Reynolds who was allowed to brew his own beer. The inn had six rooms downstairs, five upstairs and stabling for five horses.

HIGH STREET, CLAVERLEY

HIGH STREET, CLAVERLEY, *c*.1950. This pretty village of timber-framed and red sandstone houses and narrow lanes lies off the main Bridgnorth–Wolverhampton road. The name of the

village means 'the clearing where the clover grows'. The cyclists are standing outside the Kings Arms, which was licensed in about 1730. Further up the street is the Crown Inn, which was noted for its teas as well as for serving alcohol. Note the height and unusual angle of the chimney of the Crown! The landlords of both inns were summonsed in the later part of the nineteenth century for allowing drunkenness on their premises. The building between the two inns is the post office.

IN THE VILLAGE the pace of life moves quietly by and remarkably there has been very little change during the past sixty years. The chimney stack of the Crown Inn has been straightened and a few alterations made to the windows of the Kings Arms but everything else appears the same with even the water pump and stone trough still standing outside the post office. In 1901 the Crown Inn was owned and occupied by Mrs Emma Crowther who also ran a shop from there. Both the Crown Inn and the Kings Arms had a clubroom for the benefit of the locals.

BRIDGE STREET, BRIDGNORTH

BRIDGE STREET, BRIDGNORTH, *c*.1920 (right). The settlement is built on a strategic sandstone ridge high above the River Severn. In the twelfth century a bridge was erected on this site, two miles north of another crossing at Quatford, giving the town its name, Bridgnorth. In 1823 the bridge was partially rebuilt by John Smallman. He widened the roadway by adding cast-iron ribs to the third and fourth arches from the west, rebuilt one of the arches and tidied up the stonework. The bridge was widened and partially rebuilt again in 1960. The tall building to the left of the bridge is the Castle Hill Railway and Lift Vaults. In 1901 it

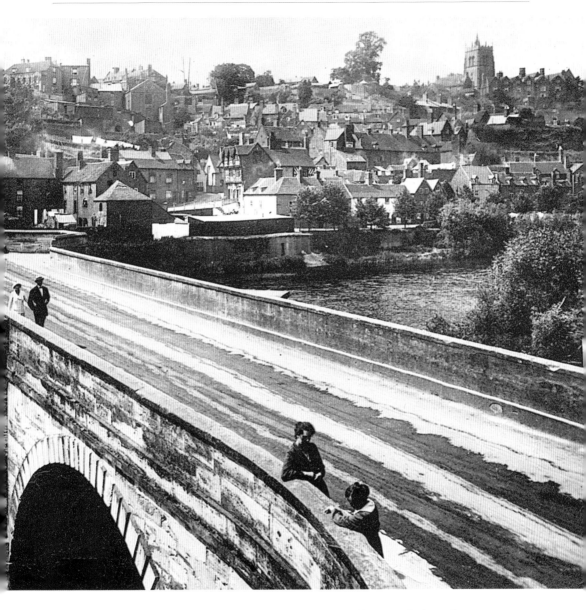

was owned by Miss Edith E. Jones of Lower Tooting, Surrey, and consisted of just three rooms on the ground floor.

ON THE RIGHT of the bridge is Ridley's Warehouse. The business was established in 1616 and advertised as the oldest firm of seedsmen in Great Britain. They sold all types of grain, clovers, grasses and roots and provided customers with quality, service and choice. They were also maltsters, using a premises in Mill Street. The advert that has adorned the side of the building for many years is now protected. The building is now occupied by a hair salon called the White Room. The Lift Vaults, which was first licensed around 1890, is still open but is now called the Severn Arms Hotel.

BRIDGNORTH

HIGH STREET, BRIDGNORTH, 1960. The Crown Hotel used to dominate this end of the High Street. It escaped the worst ravages of the 1646 fire and with the advent of the coaching era it became an important posting house and was known for a time as the Crown and Royal. Three competing companies called at the hotel with coaches travelling to Liverpool, Cheltenham, Worcester and London via Wolverhampton and Birmingham. The hotel frontage was rebuilt in

the early 1800s and during this period there was a pit for cock fighting in the yard. In 1901 there were thirty-one rooms upstairs, which included an agricultural room, a billiard room and an assembly room while on the ground floor there were nineteen rooms and stabling for thirty horses.

WOOLWORTH OPENED A store to the left of the hotel in the middle of the twentieth century. When the Crown contracted, the largest section of the hotel was converted into a new Woolworth's store; their old shop was then occupied by Superdrug. When Woolworth closed the site was taken over by the Original Factory Shop. The shop to the right of the Crown was Whitney's Bakery that was established in 1922 in St Mary's Street; it is now Catherine's Bakery. The timber-framed and red sandstone building to the left is occupied by the NatWest Bank.

HIGH STREET, CLEOBURY MORTIMER

HIGH STREET, CLEOBURY Mortimer, *c.* 1905. This small, charming market town sits on the main road from Ludlow to Bewdley. The High Street has always been the centre of trade and at the beginning of the twentieth century there were three grocers, two butchers, two drapers and clothiers, a coal merchant, a watchmaker and jeweller, a hardware store, a saddle maker, a tearoom and four boot shops. By the curb is the memorial fountain and drinking trough commemorating Captain Trow who died in South Africa during the Boer War and just to the left the stump of an

old stone cross, which is said to mark the spot where Hugh de Mortimer erected a gallows in the thirteenth century.

VERY LITTLE HAS altered apart from the chimney stacks, which have been rebuilt, and the trees, planted to commemorate Queen Victoria's Diamond Jubilee in 1897, which have been drastically cut back. Parked cars also dominate the street scene. The sign above the red car at the bottom left of the photograph is for the Talbot Inn, which has been licensed for over 200 years. The mock-Tudor frontage on the left is Victorian; it bears the initials 'E G C' and the date '1871' when it was added to mask a much older structure. The body of Prince Arthur, the elder brother of Henry VIII, was carried down this road in 1502 on its way to be interred at Worcester Cathedral after his premature death at Ludlow Castle.

LOWER BROAD STREET, LUDLOW

LOWER BROAD STREET, Ludlow, *c*.1890 (right). At the top of the street is the Broad Gate, last of the five main gateways into town. This area of town was where the poorer people involved in the town's busy cloth industry lived. Note the magnificent bell on the right, and the sign beneath that reads 'Bell Inn, R. A. Challoner. Good Stabling'. The name was transferred to this house around 1820 when the Bell in Ludford closed. A section of the building dates back to the thirteenth century and was part of St John's Hospital. The building with the two dormer windows facing down the street is the Wheatsheaf, which was first recorded in 1753.

NOW A VERY pleasant area of Ludlow to live in, the only problem being where to park your car! The Bell was closed around 1896 and is now a private residence. Note the timber-framed building above: in the old view it is a brick building but now a thin timber façade has been added in the mock-Tudor style. The Wheatsheaf is still an inn and is the last of nine public houses that once existed in this part of Ludlow. It is also reputed to be the last hostelry in the town to brew its own beer, a practice that continued up to the Second World War.

HIGH STREET, LUDLOW

HIGH STREET, LUDLOW, *c.*1935 (left). The grand building with the bell tower and clock is the Butter or Market Cross, which was erected in 1743. It was designed by William Baker of Audlem and cost in the region of £1,000. The timber-framed building on the right, standing on the corner of Broad Street, was built in the early fifteenth century and was once divided into four shops with living accommodation on the upper floors. The timber-framed building on the left dates from the late sixteenth century; the Regency style bow window was a later addition. The shop with the sunblinds was a local fishmonger's shop run by George Pearce. Note the cycle cart advertising the 'Speedy 3 Day Laundry'.

THERE HAS BEEN very little change to this scene in the last eighty years. With the exception of George Pearce's shop the rest of the buildings look the same. By the 1960s J. P. Wood occupied Pearce's shop and was advertising that they had 'never seen such an abundance of produce at such reasonable prices'. New King Edward potatoes cost 2*s* for 3lbs, frozen salmon 7*s* 6*d* a pound and a bunch of daffodils for 5*d*. Bodenham & Son moved into the timber-framed building on the corner of Broad Street by the end of the nineteenth century although the business was founded in 1863. The family are still trading there today.

CLUNTON

CLUNTON, C.1910 (right). According to the old rhyme, 'Clunton, Clunbury, Clungunford and Clun are the quietest places under the sun', and looking at both scenes you could well believe it. In the nineteenth century the village boasted a school, a post office, a Methodist church, and a pub called The Crown which all closed. The bridge is a footbridge made of wood decking and handrails on stone piers, all wagons and animals had to cross at the ford. In the 1920s the bridge attracted the attention of E. Jervoise who believed that it was quite ancient and refers to it in his book *Ancient Bridges of Wales and Western England*. The cottages at the rear often flooded during a wet winter.

THE OLD BRIDGE was demolished about 1960 and superseded by a road bridge built out of concrete with scaffolding handrails. The new bridge followed the line of the old one and used one of the piers under the main span. The bridge was mainly used by farm vehicles but by 2002 it was in a very poor condition and was replaced in the autumn of that year. The new bridge is also built out of concrete but has a strong metal girder running between the piers and a sturdy metal balustrade on each side. The cottages have also been demolished; the last people to live in the cottages were Beattie Thomas and Bert Evans. The Crown inn has been reopened by a consortium of people from the village.

THE SQUARE,
CHURCH STRETTON

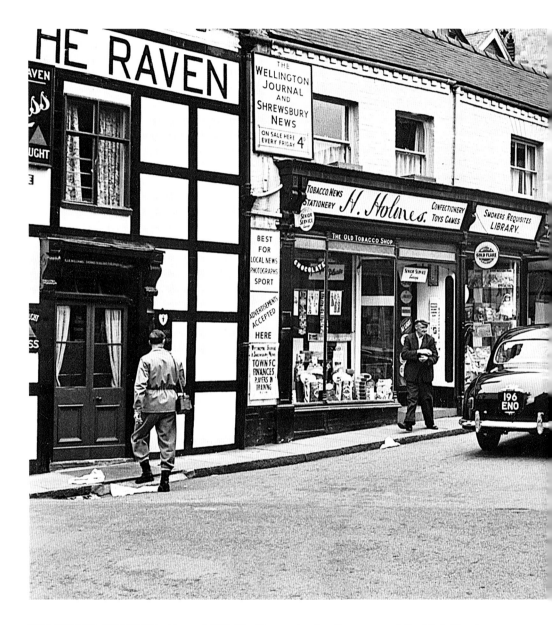

THE SQUARE, CHURCH Stretton, *c.*1958. The Raven stood on the corner of the High Street
and The Square. It was first licensed in the eighteenth century. In 1901 beer was supplied by
T. Cooper & Co. of Burton-on-Trent and custom came from passing trade and commercial

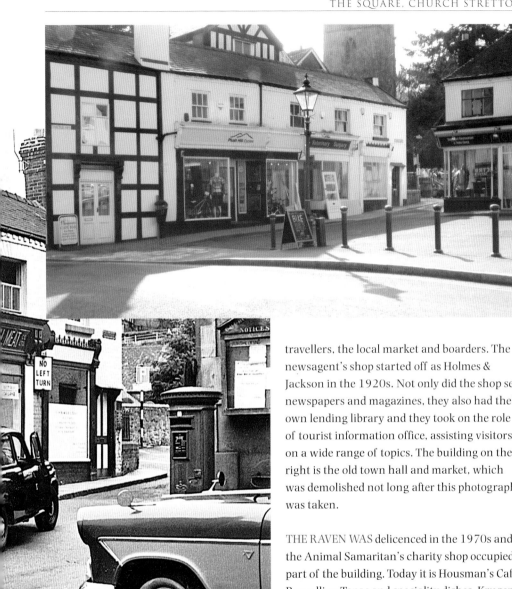

travellers, the local market and boarders. The newsagent's shop started off as Holmes & Jackson in the 1920s. Not only did the shop sell newspapers and magazines, they also had their own lending library and they took on the role of tourist information office, assisting visitors on a wide range of topics. The building on the right is the old town hall and market, which was demolished not long after this photograph was taken.

THE RAVEN WAS delicenced in the 1970s and the Animal Samaritan's charity shop occupied part of the building. Today it is Housman's Café Bar selling Tapas and speciality dishes. Kruger Tissue Group took over the newsagent's shop but after they moved out Plush Hill Cycles moved in and are advertising a bike sale on their A-board. The London Central Meat Shop who in the old view urged their customers to 'Eat More Lamb' has been converted into a veterinary surgery. The demolition of the town hall on the grounds that it was unsafe has left an open area that is still used for a weekly market and for other events. The alley between the buildings is Church Way, which leads to St Lawrence's church, whose tower can be seen over the roof line.

SANDFORD AVENUE, CHURCH STRETTON

SANDFORD AVENUE, CHURCH Stretton, 1960 (right).
This Regal Cinema was a sister to the Regal in Craven
Arms. Known as 'The Luxury Cinemas of South
Shropshire' they belonged to the Craven Cinemas Ltd.
They were advertised as air conditioned and not just
ventilated. They had luxury seating with generous leg
room, which was far in excess of the regulations. The
car and cycle parks and cloakrooms were free and the
cinemas would also supply the hard of hearing with a
free deaf aid. The interior was ornate and the walls were
covered in murals depicting Italian scenes.

BY THE 1960s television was all the rage and you could sit in the comfort of your own home and watch a variety of programmes, including films. Cinemas all over the country were shutting down and the Regal was no exception, closing its doors in 1962. The site was quickly redeveloped into a supermarket and is now occupied by Spar. Sandford Avenue takes its name from the Revd Holland Sandford, rector of Eaton-under-Haywood. He was responsible for planting the road with an avenue of lime trees, the first planted by him in December 1884. The road was formally known as Station Road.

BIRCH ROW, PONTESBURY

BIRCH ROW, PONTESBURY, *c.*1910 (right).
These very rare fourteenth-century cottages
lay off the main road through the village. It
was cruck-framed and was built as a single
dwelling. The roof was supported by massive
oak arches and the central living area had
an open hearth and a hole in the roof to let
out the smoke. Experts believed them to be
the last examples of that type of building
in England. Later the house was converted
into three cottages and by the middle of the
twentieth century the beautiful thatch was
replaced by a galvanised roof. According
to local folklore a secret passage from the
cottages to the church existed but it has
never been located.

AROUND ABOUT 1955 the cottages were
demolished and replaced by these modern

dwellings. One of the last families to live there were the Corfield family who moved into 3 Birch Row in 1948 and were there until they were taken down. When they moved into the cottage the rent was £1 4s 6d a week, but the dwelling contained no bathroom, inside toilet or running water. The wall on the left of both photographs shows the position of the photographer.

CHURCH PULVERBATCH

CHURCH PULVERBATCH, C.1900 (right). The village lies nine miles south-west of Shrewsbury on a road that runs between the Long Mynd and the Stiperstones. The White Horse Inn belonged to Trouncer's Brewery in Shrewsbury and was run by William Cox. As well as a bar and two parlours, the inn had a clubroom, six bedrooms and stabling for ten horses. Its clientele consisted mainly of agricultural workers and drovers. Another inn, the Woodcock, named after the owner W. S. Woodcock of Churton, is situated less than a hundred yards away. The village shop, belonging to Charles Powell, is situated on the corner; he was there from around 1900 to the mid 1920s.

THE INN HAS been tided up and a porch placed on the front. The cottages next door have been converted into one house and the shop has closed and been converted into a dwelling. The buildings on the opposite side of the road have been demolished and new bungalows built on the site. There are four distinct areas to the village and in 1770 this little rhyme was written about them: 'Cothercott upon the hill,/ Wilderley down in the dale,/ Churton for pretty girls,/ Pulverbatch for good ale.' Just south-west of the village is Castle Pulverbatch, the site of a Norman motte and bailey castle.

SHARPSTONES LANE, BAYSTON HILL

SHARPSTONES LANE, BAYSTON Hill, *c.* 1900. For this rural scene the photographer has his back to the A49 and is looking towards the craggy slopes of Sharpstones Hill. The hill is made up of the very hard Greywacke stone that is excellent for road building. The stone itself comes from a spur of Longmyndian rock that extends through to Bayston Hill and Sharpstones, sinks vertically down until it rises again to form the bulk of Haughmond Hill. In the past the hill was a favourite

spot for picnics as it lies just over two miles south-west of Shrewsbury. The wall in the right-hand corner is a bridge over the Shrewsbury to Hereford railway line.

THE RURAL IDYLL has gone forever. This is now Sharpstones Quarry, one of the largest in Shropshire. It has consumed most of the hill and runs for more than a kilometre along the ridge and in places is more than thirty metres deep. The quarry is owned by Tarmac and exactly the same type of stone is quarried here as is extracted on Haughmond Hill. The only feature left from the old photograph is the parapet of the railway bridge on the right. Several exciting prehistoric finds have been made in the quarry, which include the fossilised remains of an adult and two juvenile mammoths – found in 1986 – and the country's oldest man-made road, constructed by Iron Age man a hundred years before the Romans invaded Britain, which was discovered in 2011!

Other titles published by The History Press

Haunted Telford
PHILIP SOLOMON

Although it is the largest town in Shropshire, you probably wouldn't think there would be many ghosts lurking in the new town of Telford. However, Telford plays host to many spirits from the past. From heart-stopping accounts of apparitions, manifestations and related supernatural phenomena to first-hand encounters with spirits, this collection of stories contains both new and well-known spooky stories from in and around Telford. It is sure to fascinate everyone with an interest in the area's history.

978 0 7524 5766 6

Haunted Shropshire
ALLAN SCOTT-DAVIES

Haunted Shropshire is a tour through one of the most haunted counties in the UK. It has stories that will make you scared such as the one about the moving road on Wenlock Edge; it may move you to tears when you hear the tale of Madam Pigott and how cruelly she was treated. It may make you laugh at the story of the kissing maid in Market Drayton and intrigued by the story of the Black Lady of Bridgnorth. This book will open up your eyes to the vast number of ghosts who wander the hills, streets, buildings and even lakes of Shropshire.

978 0 7524 4787 2

Shropshire Folk Tales
AMY DOUGLAS

The thirty stories in *Shropshire Folk Tales* have grown out of the county's diverse landscapes: tales of the strange and the macabre; memories of magic and other worlds; proud recollections of folk history; stories to make you smile, sigh and shiver. Moulded by the land, weather and generations of tongues wagging, these traditional tales are full of Shropshire wit and wisdom, and will be enjoyed time and again.

978 0 7524 5155 8

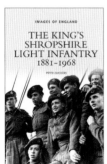

The King's Shropshire Light Infantry
PETER DUCKERS

Peter Duckers' book presents a photographic record of the service of a distinguished county regiment whose origins go back to the Seven Years' War, in the middle of the eighteenth century. This fascinating book presents a vivid picture of the life of the regiment in times of peace and war through photographs from the regimental archives, the majority of which have never before been published.

978 0 7524 1193 4

Visit our website and discover thousands of other History Press books.

www.thehistorypress.co.uk